The Annexation of Texas

From Republic to Statehood

Joanne Mattern

Consultant

Julie Hyman, MS.Ed.
Social Studies Coordinator
Birdville ISD

Publishing Credits

Dona Herweck Rice, *Editor-in-Chief*
Lee Aucoin, *Creative Director*
Marcus McArthur, Ph.D., *Associate Education Editor*
Neri Garcia, *Senior Designer*
Stephanie Reid, *Photo Editor*
Rachelle Cracchiolo, M.S.Ed., *Publisher*

Image Credits:
Cover State Preservation Board, Austin, Texas & LOC [LC-USZC4-2957]; p.1 State Preservation Board, Austin, Texas; pp.2–3 LOC [LC-USZC4-2957]; p.4 Bridgeman Art Library; p.5 North Wind Picture Archives; p.5 (sidebar) Wikimedia; p.6 Bridgeman Art Library; p.7 Texas State Library and Archives; p.7 (sidebar) The Portal to Texas History; p.8 Bridgeman Art Library; p.9 North Wind Picture Archives; p.9 (sidebar) LOC [LC-USZ62-27732]; p.10 North Wind Picture Archives; p.11 Texas State Library and Archives ; p.12 Star of the Republic Museum; p.13 (top) Bridgeman Art Library; p.14 North Wind Picture Archives; p.15 (top) San Jacinto Museum of History, (bottom) U.S. Navy Department/UNT Libraries; p.16–17 Image courtesy of William Adams and the Texas Ranger Hall of Fame and Museum; p.17 (sidebar) Alamy; p.18 The Granger Collection; p.19 The Granger Collection; p.20 Corbis; p.21 (top) DeGolyer Library; p.22 LOC [LC-USZ62-839482]; p.23 Bridgeman Art Library; p.24 (left) State Preservation Board, Austin, Texas; p.24 (right) LOC [LC-rbpe-1190260a]; p.25 The White House Historical Association; p.26 Bridgeman Art Library; p.27 North Wind Picture Archives; p.28 The Granger Collection; p.29 North Wind Picture Archives; p.32 LOC [LC-rbpe-1190260a]; All other images Shutterstock.

Teacher Created Materials
5301 Oceanus Drive
Huntington Beach, CA 92649-1030
http://www.tcmpub.com

ISBN 978-1-4333-5048-1

Table of Contents

A Long Journey

Texas has seen many changes during its history. At first, American Indians roamed through Texas land. When European explorers arrived in Texas, they claimed the land for Spain. Then in 1821, Texas became part of Mexico.

Mexico wanted people to settle the area. It invited people from the United States to move to Texas in exchange for land. But these American **colonists**, or settlers, did not like the way Mexico treated them. American settlers and Mexican-born **Tejanos** (tay-HA-noz) wanted to make their own rules.

Spanish explorers land in the New World.

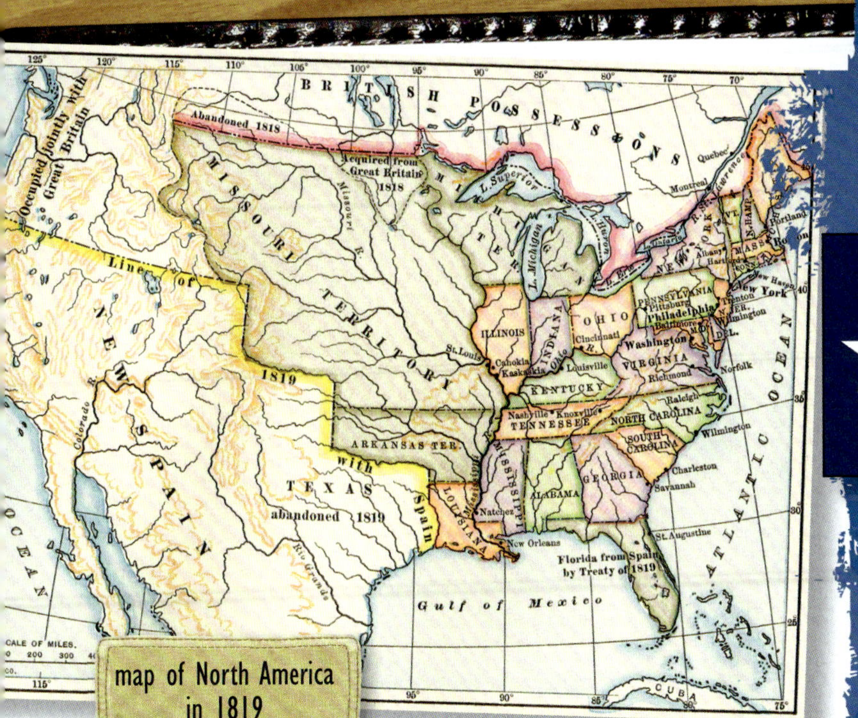

map of North America in 1819

By the 1830s, people living in Texas were ready to go to war for their freedom. After a short but bloody war, Texas won its independence. Now, Texas was a **republic**. It was a separate country with its own government.

The Republic of Texas faced many problems. It had many strong leaders, but most of these leaders knew that Texas needed help. Some of them looked to the United States for help, but they did not all agree that joining the United States would solve their problems.

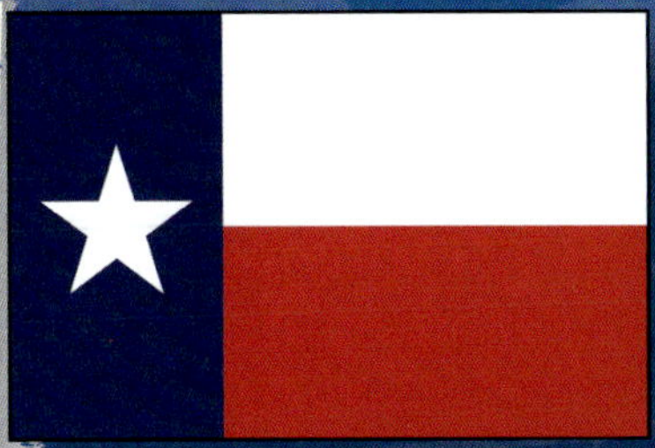

Lone Star Flag

The Texas flag was adopted in 1838. It includes red, white, and blue stripes and a single white star on the left side. Blue stands for loyalty, white for purity, and red for bravery. The star stands for the unity of Texas when it declared independence from Mexico. When Texas became a state, it kept the same flag it had when it was a republic.

Tejanos

Tejanos were Mexicans who lived in Texas. Historians use this term to distinguish American-born Texans from Mexican-born Texans, expecially during the Texas **Revolution**.

Fighting for Freedom

Texas vs. Mexico

In 1835, new Mexican president Antonio López de Santa Anna (ahn-TOH-nee-oh LOH-pehs deh sahn-tah AH-nah) was worried there were too many Americans living in Texas. So he outlawed American **immigration** to Texas. Santa Anna also made Americans pay higher taxes. Most Americans felt that Santa Anna was unfair. They were worried that things would only get worse. They decided to fight for their freedom.

On October 2, 1835, Texas and Mexico fought at the Battle of Gonzales. The Texas soldiers defeated the Mexican Army. But the Battle of Gonzales would only be the first fight in a bloody war for Texas independence.

While soldiers fought, the leaders of Texas were busy. In February 1836, Texans elected **delegates**. These people represented Texas at a **convention**. On March 1, these 59 men met in Washington-on-the-Brazos. They had to work quickly because Mexican soldiers were headed their way.

Santa Anna leads the Mexican Army.

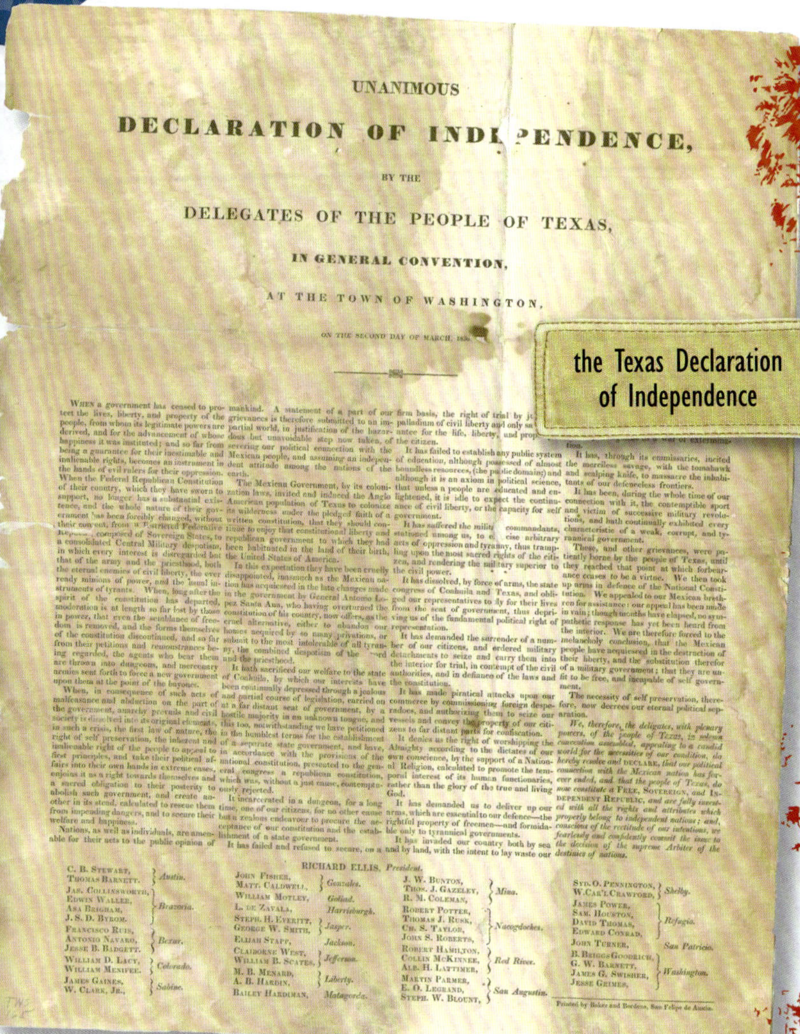

UNANIMOUS

DECLARATION OF INDEPENDENCE,

BY THE

DELEGATES OF THE PEOPLE OF TEXAS,

IN GENERAL CONVENTION,

AT THE TOWN OF WASHINGTON,

the Texas Declaration of Independence

At the convention, the delegates wrote the Texas Declaration of Independence. It declared that Texas was a free republic. The men also elected leaders to serve until they could hold elections. They chose David G. Burnet to be the **interim** president of Texas.

Stephen F. Austin

First Army of Texas

Texas did not have an army when the Mexicans attacked in the Battle of Gonzales. The soldiers at Gonzales were volunteers who fought for their freedom and their homes. After the battle, Stephen F. Austin formed and led the First Army of Texas Volunteers.

A Good Model

The Texas Declaration of Independence is based on the United States Declaration of Independence. Like the American version, the Texas Declaration explained why it was becoming a separate republic. Five men wrote the Texas Declaration in less than a day.

A Terrible War

Texas claimed to be a free country, but it still had to win its freedom in battle. In March 1836, Texas faced two terrible defeats. The first came on March 6 at an old **mission** called *the Alamo*. After a **siege** that lasted 13 days, the Mexicans burst into the Alamo and killed nearly every man inside. A few weeks later, the Mexican Army defeated the Texans at a place called *Goliad* (GO-lee-ad).

Sam Houston (far left) charges Mexican troops.

Texas needed a hero to rally Texans for the cause of freedom. They found one in Sam Houston. Houston led an army to the eastern part of Texas where his men met Santa Anna's forces. The two armies fought at the Battle of San Jacinto (sahn ha-SEEN-toh) on April 21. Houston easily defeated the Mexicans and captured Santa Anna.

Many people thought Santa Anna should be killed, but Houston and the other Texas leaders let him go. On May 14, Santa Anna signed the **Treaty** of Velasco (beh-LAHS-koh). The treaty ended the war with Texas. Santa Anna was given his freedom after signing the treaty, but he did not keep his word. Santa Anna hoped to make Texas part of Mexico again.

Mexican soldiers set the Alamo on fire.

Sam Houston

Sam Houston

Sam Houston was born in Virginia in 1793. During his life, he lived with the Cherokee (CHER-uh-kee) American Indians and was governor of Tennessee. He also served as a U. S. Representative from Tennessee. Then, he became a war hero and later the second president of Texas. After Texas joined the United States, he served as the state's governor. Many consider Houston to be one of the great heroes of Texas history.

A New Republic

The First Presidents

David G. Burnet led Texas until the republic held an election. On October 22, 1836, Sam Houston became the first elected president of the Texas Republic. Mirabeau Lamar (MIR-uh-boh luh-MAHR) had fought at the Battle of San Jacinto with Houston. Lamar was voted to be Houston's vice president, but the two men had very different ideas about how to run the new republic.

Sam Houston

The Texas Republic faced many problems. It had huge **debts** and had trouble with American Indians. Houston wanted to make peace treaties with the tribes in Texas. Mexico proved to be another problem. Houston knew Mexico would continue to cause trouble. Houston wanted Texas to join the United States because he believed that being part of the United States would give Texas the best chance to survive.

Lamar had very different ideas. He did not want to sign peace treaties with the American Indians. Instead, he wanted to chase them out of the republic. Lamar also wanted Texas to stay independent because he did not think the republic needed to join the United States. Rather, he wanted Texas to get bigger and stretch all the way to the Pacific Ocean!

Texas capitol in Austin

Four Presidents

Texas had four presidents in the time between independence and statehood. Burnet served the shortest term—only seven months. Sam Houston was the only president to serve two terms.

Where Is the Capital?

The Texas capital moved around a lot during the first year of the republic. During 1836, the capital was located in Washington-on-the-Brazos, Harrisburg, Galveston, Velasco, and Columbia. Then, it moved to Houston for two years. The capital finally moved to Austin in 1839. It moved so many times because the Texas government was trying to avoid the Mexican Army.

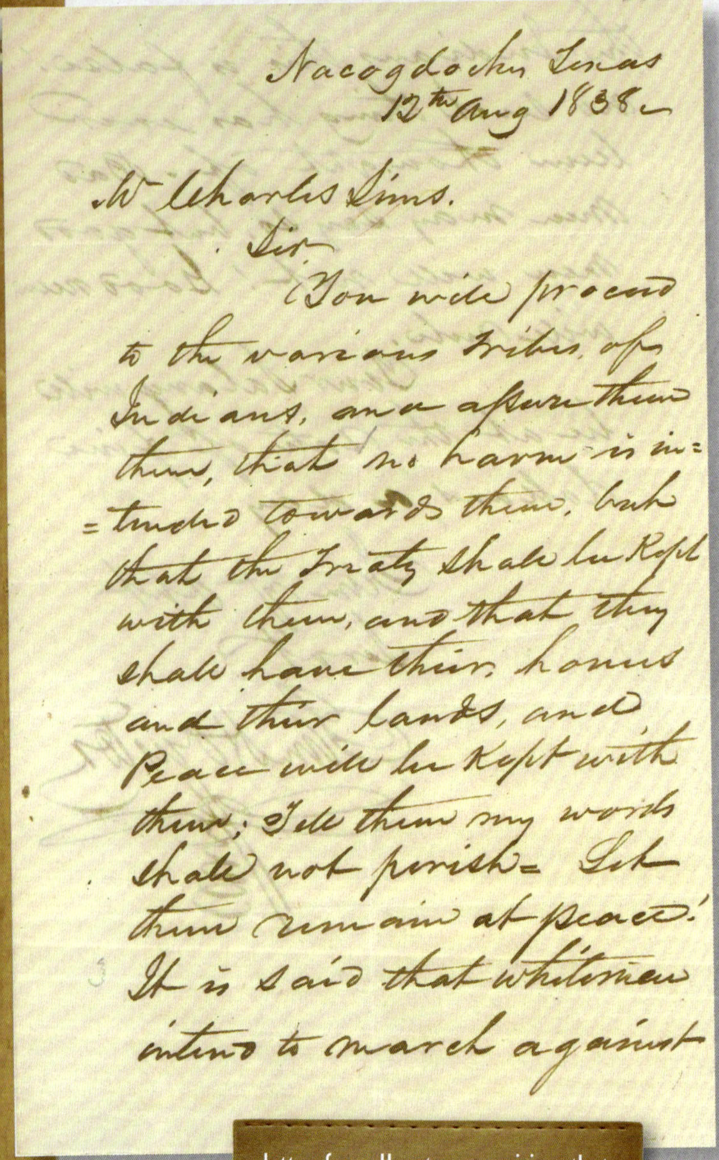
Nacogdoches Texas
12th Aug 1838

Mr Charles Sims.

Sir,

You will proceed to the various tribes of Indians, and assure them, that no harm is intended towards them, but that the Treaty shall be kept with them, and that they shall have their homes and their lands, and Peace will be kept with them; Tell them my words shall not perish= Let them remain at peace! It is said that whitemen intend to march against

letter from Houston promising that the Cherokee would keep their land

Rebellion!

There were many American Indian tribes in Texas. President Houston did his best to keep peace with them. He made treaties with many tribes, but he was mostly worried about the Cherokee. The Cherokee had settled on good land in East Texas. Houston promised they could stay on that land and asked the Texas Senate to approve a treaty between Texas and the Cherokee. But the Senate rejected his request.

In the summer of 1838, some people in an East Texas town called *Nacogdoches* (nak-uh-DOH-chuhz) discovered a plot known as the *Cordova Rebellion*.

Texas Rangers, 1845

The Cherokee were angry that Texas did not keep its promise to give the tribe their land. They met with a judge in Nacogdoches named Vicente Cordova (bee-SEN-teh core-DOH-bah). He created a secret treaty with Mexico. Cordova promised that the Cherokee would attack the Texas colonists and help Mexico reclaim Texas. In return, Mexico promised to give the Cherokee their land.

Texas leaders discovered the plot. There were several battles between the Cherokee and the Texas Rangers. Texas captured some of the rebels and tried them for **treason**. The Cordova Rebellion was over, but trouble between Texas and the Cherokee did not end.

The Cherokee

The Cherokee lived in what are now the states of Georgia, Tennessee, North Carolina, South Carolina, Alabama, Kentucky, Virginia, and West Virginia. Over time, the U.S. government forced them to move. Some settled in Texas, but later they were forced to move to present-day Oklahoma.

The Texas Rangers

Stephen F. Austin founded the Texas Rangers in 1823. He hired 10 men to protect hundreds of families who moved to Texas after Mexico became independent from Spain. In 1835, the Texas Rangers became a formal organization.

The Fight Over Statehood

Different Ideas

Sam Houston was president of Texas from 1836 to 1838. Texas law said the president could not serve two terms in a row, so Mirabeau Lamar became the new president in 1838. Lamar wanted Texas to stretch all the way west to the Pacific Ocean. He also wanted Texas to start a national bank and free public schools.

Lamar knew it was important to protect Texas's borders. He wanted to build military posts along the border with Mexico. He also said Texas needed a navy that would protect Texan ships at sea.

One of Lamar's main goals was to remove American Indians from Texas. Sam Houston wanted to be friends with the American Indians, but Lamar did not. Lamar said that tribes had no rights to any land in Texas. He forced most of the American Indians out of the region. Houston's Cherokee friends were forced to move to Oklahoma.

Lamar also disagreed with Houston about joining the United States. He believed Texas could be a great and powerful nation on its own.

Mirabeau Lamar

The *Independence* was a ship in the Texas Navy.

CAPTURE OF THE INDEPENDENCE

IV. Ships of the Texas Navy

Name	Type	Origin	Commissioned	Tonnage	Length	Beam	Draft	Crew[1]	Guns	Disposition
Independence (Ingham).[2]	Ex-U.S. Revenue Cutter.	Purchased New Orleans.	Early 1836	150	80'	x[3]	x	9-11	Small guns	Captured off Galveston, 17 April 1837.
Brutus	Schooner	Purchased New Orleans.	February 1836	160	approx. 180'	x	x	40	1 18-pdr. swivel; 9 smaller guns.	Wrecked off Galveston, 27 August 1837.
Liberty (William Robbins).	Schooner	Purchased Galveston.	9 January 1836	70	x	x	x	20-50	6 small guns	Sold at New Orleans, 1837.
Invincible	Schooner	Purchased Galveston.	Early 1836	100	x	x	x	40	1 9-pdr. swivel; 6 carronades.	Wrecked off Galveston, 27 August 1837.
Potomac	Ex-merchant brig.	Purchased Galveston.	1838	x	x	x	x	Served as station and receiving ship at Galveston.		Apparently never left Galveston.
Zavala (Charleston).	Steamship-of-War.	Philadelphia; purchased 1837 & armed.	23 March 1839	569	201'	24'	12'	24 officers, 102 enlisted.	4 12-pdr. medium; 1 9-pdr. long.	Run ashore at Galveston, June, 1842; sold for scrap, June, 1843.
San Jacinto (Viper).	Schooner	Built in Baltimore.	27 June 1839	170	66'	21'6"	8'	13 officers, 69 enlisted.	4 12-pdr. medium; 1 9-pdr. long pivot.	Damaged at Arcas Island, 31 October 1840; wrecked by a gale there 25 November 1840.
San Antonio (Asp).	Schooner	Built in Baltimore.	7 August 1839	170	66'	21'6"	8'	13 officers, 69 enlisted.	Same as *San Jacinto*.	Lost at sea, September 1842.
San Bernard (Scorpion).	Schooner	Built in Baltimore.	31 August 1839	170	66'	21'6"	8'	13 officers, 69 enlisted.	Same as *San Jacinto*.	Beached at Galveston, September 1842; repaired, transferred to U.S. Navy, 11 May 1846; sold for $150, 30 November 1846.
Louisville (Striped Pig).	Schooner (tender).	x	Bought 25 Sept. 1839.	95	x	x	x	x	x	x.
Wharton (Colorado).	Brig	Built in Baltimore.	Delivered 18 Oct. 1839.	405	110'	28'	11'	17 officers, 123 enlisted.	15 18-pdrs. medium; 1 12-pdr. long.	Transferred to U.S. Navy, 11 May 1846; sold to Galveston for $55, 30 November 1846.
Austin (Texas)	Sloop-of-War	Built in Baltimore.	5 January 1840	600	125'	31'	12'6"	23 officers, 151 enlisted.	16 24-pdr. medium; 2 18-pdr. medium; 2 18-pdr. long.	Transferred to U.S. Navy 11 May 1846; towed to Pensacola; run aground and broken up, 1848.
Archer (Galveston) (Brazos).	Brig	Built in Baltimore.	25 April 1840	400	110'	28'	11'	17 officers, 123 enlisted.	14 18-pdr. medium.	Transferred to U.S. Navy, 11 May 1846; sold for $450, 30 November 1846.

[1] Crew figures indicate complement if fully manned.
[2] Names in parentheses indicate other names by which the vessel was known in her career.
[3] Unknown or unavailable information is indicated by an "x."

This chart shows the ships employed by the Texas Navy.

Mirabeau Lamar

Mirabeau Lamar was born in Georgia in 1798. He moved to Texas in 1835. Lamar became a hero at the Battle of San Jacinto. He was the Texas secretary of war before becoming vice president under Sam Houston. Lamar died in 1859.

The Texas Navy

Texas has had two navies. The first navy was formed in 1836 and had four ships. These ships blocked supply routes to Santa Anna's army and helped Texas win its independence. In 1839, a second navy was formed. When Texas joined the United States, its ships became part of the U. S. Navy.

Death at the Council House

For years, Texas settlers and Comanche (kuh-MAN-chee) tribes had fought over land. By 1840, the Comanche had been weakened by **smallpox** and attacks by the Texas Rangers. Several members of the tribes went to San Antonio to meet with Texas leaders. Texas demanded that the Comanche return all prisoners, leave central Texas, and stay away from all white settlers.

On March 19, the Comanche members arrived in San Antonio. They met in a building called the *Council House*. The Comanche were only able to bring a few prisoners with them. This was because other **bands** held the other prisoners. The Texas leaders said they would hold the Comanche hostage until all the prisoners were released.

The Comanche tried to escape from the Council House, and a fierce battle followed. Texas soldiers killed 35 Comanche and held the other 29 Comanche members as prisoners.

The Council House Fight made the Comanche very angry. To get back at Texas, they led a **raid** that swept through the Guadalupe River valley. During the raid, they wore stolen hats and clothing.

The Comanche seek revenge after the Council House Fight in 1840.

Smallpox spreads throughout an American Indian village.

Smallpox

When European explorers came to America, they brought diseases like smallpox with them. The disease wiped out entire American Indian tribes who had no resistance to smallpox and could not fight off the infection.

Misunderstood

The Comanche chief could not give up the Texas prisoners. Other Comanche bands held these prisoners, and he could not tell them what to do. The chief was not the chief of those Comanche bands. The Texas leaders did not understand this. They thought the Comanche chief was lying.

The Trip to Santa Fe

There were many settlers living west of Texas in New Mexico, which was part of Mexico at the time. Lamar wanted Texas to expand westward. He said that these settlers should become part of Texas. If New Mexico joined Texas, then Texas would control important trade routes that ran through the area. Lamar wanted to control the Santa Fe Trail because it was the most important route to the west.

Lamar wrote a letter to the governor of New Mexico inviting the Mexican territory to become part of Texas. The governor never answered his letter, but Lamar refused to give up. He decided to send a group of men to New Mexico to convince the region to join Texas.

The Santa Fe Expedition observes an American Indian bison hunt.

Santa Fe Trail

In June 1841, the Santa Fe **Expedition** left for New Mexico. The long journey through the desert was very hard. The group did not reach Santa Fe until September. They thought the residents would welcome them. Instead, they got a big surprise! New Mexico's governor had sent an army to stop the expedition. The members of the expedition surrendered. They were taken prisoner and sent to Mexico. They did not return home until April 1842.

The Way West

The Santa Fe Trail was the main route from Missouri to Mexico and the Southwest. Thousands of people and supplies made their way across the Santa Fe Trail. Later, this route became part of the railroad that linked the eastern United States and the western United States.

Mexico or Texas?

New Mexico was originally part of the Spanish territory called ***New Spain***. It became part of Mexico in 1821. Although Texas claimed some of the land, New Mexico remained under Mexican rule until 1848.

New Friends, Old Foes

Lamar's term as president ended in 1841. Texas had many debts, they were still fighting with Mexico, and many people in Texas were unhappy. In 1841, Sam Houston ran for president again and won.

Houston's goal was to make Texas a strong republic. He met with leaders of other countries and asked them to recognize Texas as a free republic. France and Great Britain agreed. The two countries signed official treaties with Texas. Now, other countries knew that France and Great Britain would help Texas if it were in trouble.

Sam Houston

Texas was still in debt, so Houston took out loans from American banks. He also took property from Mexicans to help pay some of Texas's debts. Slowly, the Texas Republic grew stronger. However, the republic still had an old problem—Mexico.

Santa Anna

In October 1841, Santa Anna became president of Mexico for the second time. He was determined to make Texas part of Mexico again. In 1842, Santa Anna sent an army into Texas. On March 5, Rafael Vásquez (rah-fah-EL BAHS-kehs) led a Mexican army of around 700 men into San Antonio. The Texans knew they could not win the battle and left the city without a fight. Having successfully captured the city, Vásquez left San Antonio two days later. But Adrian Woll would march another Mexican army into San Antonio later that year.

Broken Promise

Many people thought Santa Anna should have been killed after Houston captured him at the Battle of San Jacinto. Instead, Houston let Santa Anna go after he promised to stop fighting with Texas. But, Santa Anna did not keep his promise.

A Frenchman

Adrian Woll fought for Mexico, but he was not Mexican. Woll was born in France. He came to the United States and eventually moved to Mexico. After a long military career there, he moved back to France, where he died in 1875.

Adrian Woll

The Fighting Continues

On September 11, 1842, General Woll and 1,400 troops marched into San Antonio. After the first invasion by Vásquez, Captain Matthew Caldwell had raised an army of 225 volunteer Texans. His army met with Captain John C. Hays's army of 14 at Salado (suh-LAH-doh) Creek. This was about 7 miles (11 km) outside San Antonio. There, the two armies devised a plan. Hays's men would lure the Mexican troops out of San Antonio and into Salado (suh-LAH-doh) Creek. There the Texans would be ready and waiting. The plan worked! The Texans were able to attack successfully and later chase away the Mexican Army.

Captain John C. Hays

Texan soldiers draw beans after the failed Mier Expedition.

In December 1842, President Houston sent soldiers to the area under General Alexander Somervell. Somervell captured the Mexican towns of Laredo and Guerrero. Most of the Texans returned home because they did not have enough supplies, but a group of more than 300 men refused to leave. They marched along the Rio Grande to the town of Mier (mee-AIHR). They ordered the people of Mier to give them food and supplies.

The Mexican Army rushed to defend Mier. The Mexican Army was 10 times bigger than the Texas forces. The Texas soldiers had no choice but to surrender.

Deadly Lottery

After the Mier Expedition, Mexican leaders ordered every tenth Texan prisoner to be executed. They decided to hold a **lottery** to decide which men would die. The men drew beans out of a large bowl. Those who drew white beans were spared. Those who picked black beans were shot to death.

Dawson Massacre

Captain Nicholas M. Dawson had also raised an army of 53 Texans. Dawson believed that Caldwell's men were in grave danger. He quickly marched his army toward Salado Creek to help. But his men were cut off by 500 Mexican soldiers. Dawson's men fought bravely but in the end were outnumbered. Two men escaped, 15 were taken prisoner, and 36 were killed.

a poster announcing a meeting of New Yorkers against annexation

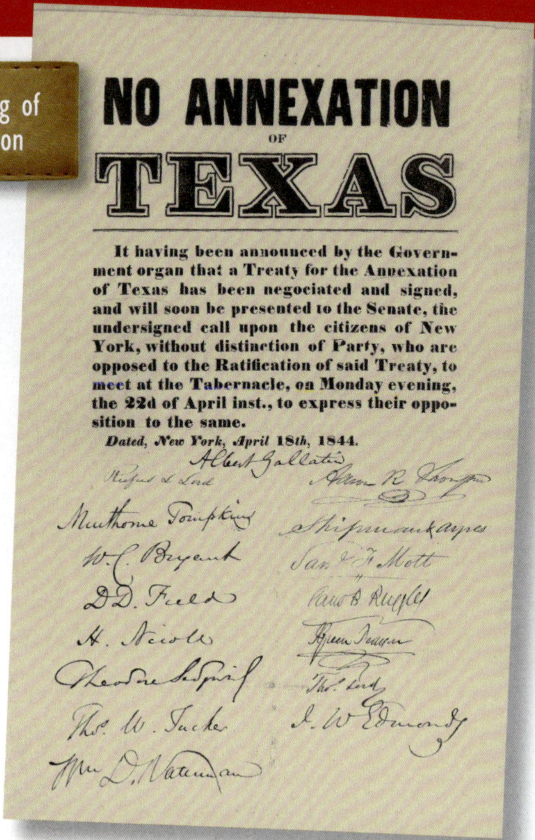

NO ANNEXATION OF TEXAS

It having been announced by the Government organ that a Treaty for the Annexation of Texas has been negociated and signed, and will soon be presented to the Senate, the undersigned call upon the citizens of New York, without distinction of Party, who are opposed to the Ratification of said Treaty, to meet at the Tabernacle, on Monday evening, the 22d of April inst., to express their opposition to the same.

Dated, New York, April 18th, 1844.

Anson Jones

A State at Last!

"The Republic of Texas Is No More"

In 1844, Anson (AN-suhn) Jones became president of Texas. Both Jones and Houston wanted the United States to **annex**, or add, Texas to the country. Jones knew the United States would protect Texas from Mexico.

President John Tyler and the U. S. Congress supported annexing Texas. They liked that Texas would add a lot of land to the United States. And they knew that Great Britain was trying to block annexation and U. S. expansion west. Plus, Texas would enter the Union as a slave state. This was important to Southerners. They wanted slavery to extend into the western territories. But Northerners who were against slavery did not approve of Texas being annexed as a slave state.

Tyler signed the **joint resolution** annexing Texas on March 1, 1845. But the Texas Congress still had to agree to join the United States. By this time, the Mexican government had offered to recognize the Republic of Texas. But Texas leaders were determined to join the United States. On July 4, the day Americans celebrated their independence, the Texas Congress agreed to join the United States.

By the time Texas agreed to annexation, James K. Polk was the new U. S. president. On December 29, 1845, Polk welcomed Texas as the 28th state. Texas had been a republic for just under 10 years.

James K. Polk

Not So Fast!

Mexico did not like the idea of Texas becoming part of the United States. Mexico sent a peace treaty to Texas just before Texas voted to join the United States. But Texas was not interested and never signed the treaty. On December 19, 1846, President Jones transferred his power to Texas Governor James Pinckney Henderson. Jones said, "The final act in this great drama is now performed; the Republic of Texas is no more."

Not the Only One

Texas was not the only state to be a free republic before joining the United States. Vermont was independent until it joined the United States in 1791. Hawaii was both a kingdom and a republic before it became the 50th state in 1959.

The Mexican-American War

Mexico was angry that the United States had annexed Texas. Mexico and the United States also did not agree on the border between Texas and Mexico. The United States said it was the Rio Grande. Mexico said the border was farther north at the Nueces (noo-EY-suhs) River.

President Polk secretly sent U.S. **agent** John Slidell to Mexico City to make a treaty with Mexican leaders. Polk wanted to buy the entire territory west to the Pacific Ocean for $30 million. When Slidell arrived, the Mexican president refused to see him.

Mexico's army attacked American soldiers near the Rio Grande. Polk asked Congress to declare war against Mexico. Polk told Congress that Mexico had "invaded our territory and shed American blood on American soil." In May 1846, Congress declared war on Mexico. This marked the beginning of the Mexican-American war.

American troops occupy Mexico City after the Mexican-American War.

This map shows the land the United States received from Mexico after the war.

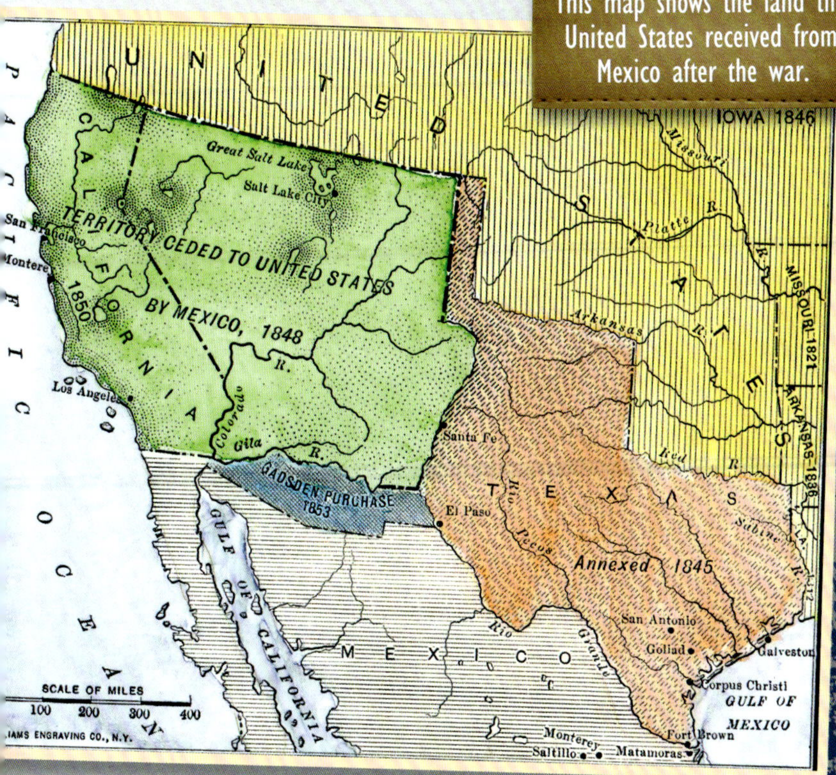

The war did not last long. The United States was far more powerful than Mexico. On February 2, 1848, Mexico and the United States signed the Treaty of Guadalupe Hidalgo (gwahd-l-OOP-ay hi-DAHL-goh). This treaty said that the border between Texas and Mexico was the Rio Grande. The treaty also let the United States purchase the land west of Texas for $15 million.

What a Deal!

After the war, the United States bought land from Mexico through the Treaty of Guadalupe Hidalgo. For half the price they were willing to pay before the war, the United States bought all of the land west to the Pacific Ocean. That land is now the states of California, Nevada, Utah, and parts of Colorado, New Mexico, and Arizona.

Even More Land!

In 1853, just five years after the war, the United States bought even more land from Mexico. The Gadsden (GADZ-duhn) Purchase gave the United States the southern parts of New Mexico and Arizona. They paid Mexico $10 million for the land.

The U.S. Senate debates the Compromise of 1850.

A State United, A Nation Divided

In the first half of the 1800s, slavery split the United States. Many Northerners were against slavery. But most Southerners supported it. New states were forming in the western territories. It was time for the country to decide if slavery would be allowed in these new states.

Southern states said they would **secede** (si-SEED), or withdraw, from the Union if they were not allowed to bring their slaves into western states. To stop them, the United States passed the **Compromise** of 1850. The Compromise said that the United States would give Texas millions of dollars to help pay its debts. Texas was to give up its claim to New Mexico. Slavery would only be allowed in parts of the western territories.

The Compromise of 1850 did not keep the peace for long. In 1861, 11 Southern states seceded from the United States. They formed a new country called the *Confederate States of America,* or the **Confederacy**. Texas left the United States and joined the Confederacy. The American Civil War had begun.

Texas's path from Mexican territory to American statehood was paved with challenges. Many Texan heroes gave their lives for independence and statehood.

Dividing Line

The line that divided North from South was called the *Mason-Dixon Line*. This line was first drawn in the 1760s to end a border argument between British colonies. The line was named after the two men who studied the map and drew the line.

Population Boom

Texas had about 50,000 people when the republic started in 1836. By 1848, its population had grown to more than 158,000. The population of Texas has continued to grow ever since.

an 1861 map showing the seceding states

Glossary

agent—a person who acts or does business for another

annex—take over a territory and make it part of a larger territory

bands—small family groups

colonists—people who start a colony or settle an area

compromise—an agreement between people who have given up some of their demands

Confederacy—the government of the Southern states that seceded from the United States between 1861 and 1865

convention—a meeting to discuss common concerns

debts—money owed to another person or people

delegates—people who represent other people at a meeting

expedition—a trip made for a specific purpose, especially to explore

immigration—the act of moving to a new country

interim—temporary

joint resolution—a resolution or declaration agreed upon by the U. S. Senate and House and then approved by the president

lottery—a gambling contest where tickets are sold and prizes are given to a ticket that is randomly chosen

mission—religious and military outpost established by the Spanish during colonization

New Spain—areas claimed by Spain that included Mexico and the Southwest United States

raid—to attack suddenly; to steal or destroy property

republic—a political system in which people elect representatives to make laws for them

revolution—an act of overthrowing and replacing one government with another

secede—to leave a country and form a new government

siege—a military strategy in which troops surround an area and cut off outside access to force a surrender

smallpox—a disease caused by a virus; characterized by a fever and skin rash

Tejanos—Mexican-born Texans

treason—the crime of betraying or fighting against your own government

treaty—a legal agreement between two governments

Index

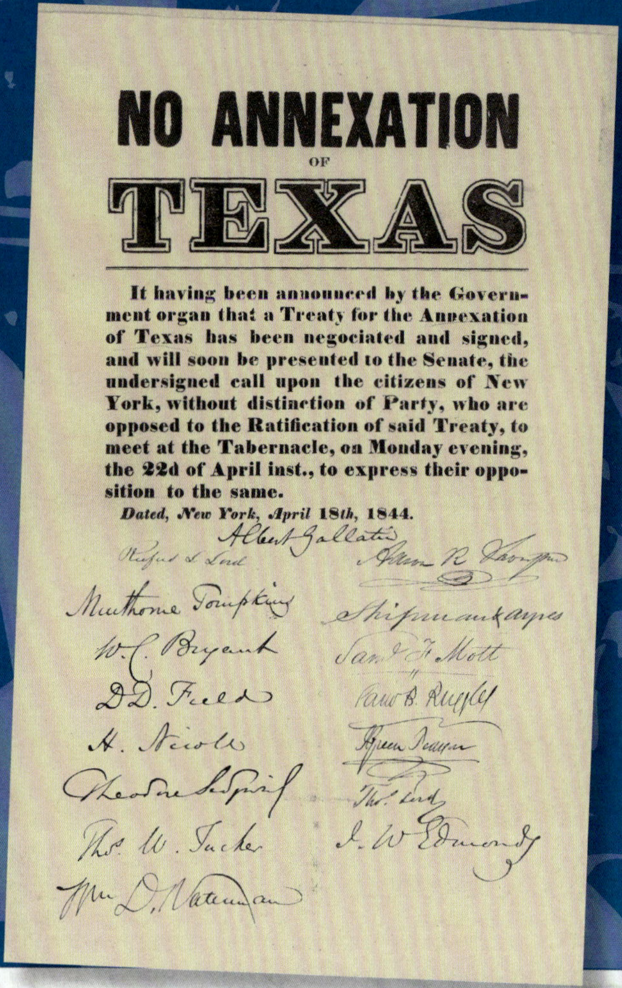

NO ANNEXATION OF TEXAS

It having been announced by the Government organ that a Treaty for the Annexation of Texas has been negociated and signed, and will soon be presented to the Senate, the undersigned call upon the citizens of New York, without distinction of Party, who are opposed to the Ratification of said Treaty, to meet at the Tabernacle, on Monday evening, the 22d of April inst., to express their opposition to the same.

Dated, New York, April 18th, 1844.

Your Turn!

In 1844, there was much debate over whether Texas should join the United States. U.S. President John Tyler supported annexation. But many northerners were against Texas being annexed as a slave state.

To Annex or Not to Annex?

Write a catchy slogan in support of or against the annexation of Texas.